nd a confidant. I'm not ashamed to say, I hope it always will stay this way, ... won't

the biggest gift would be from me, and the card attac... ... ng a

ight. I'm not ashamed to say, I hope it always will stay th... ...ds off, won't you stand

even though it's hard to hear, I will stand real close and say, thank you for being a friend. And

our name, then once again... thank you for being a friend. Thank you for being a friend, travelled

ay, I hope it always will stay this way, my hat is off, won't you stand up and take a bow. And if

the card attached would say, thank you for being a friend. If it's a car you lack, I'd surely buy

lways will stay this way, my hat is off, won't you stand up and take a bow. And when we both

d real close and say, thank you for being a friend. And when we die, and float away, into the

u for being a friend. Thank you for being a friend, travelled down a road and back again, your

, my hat is off, won't you stand up and take a bow. And if you threw a party, invited everyone

k you for being a friend. If it's a car you lack, I'd surely buy you a Cadillac, whatever you need

ff, won't you stand up and take a bow. And when we both get older, with walking canes and

being a friend. And when we die, and float away, into the night, the Milky Way, you'll hear me

r being a friend, travelled down a road and back again, your heart is true, you're a pal and a

up and take a bow. And if you threw a party, invited everyone you knew, you would see, the

a car you lack, I'd surely buy you a Cadillac, whatever you need any time of the day or night.

e a bow. And when we both get older, with walking canes and hair of grey, have no fear even

ie, and float away, into the night, the Milky Way, you'll hear me call, as we ascend, I'll say your

road and back again, your heart is true, you're a pal and a confidant. I'm not ashamed to say,

w a party, invited everyone you knew, you would see, the biggest gift would be from me, and

Cadillac, whatever you need any time of the day or night. I'm not ashamed to say, I hope it

der, with walking canes and hair of grey, have no fear even though it's hard to hear, I will stand

Milky Way, you'll hear me call, as we ascend, I'll say your name, then once again... thank you

1/7/06

A gift for:

Tessi ♡

From:

Maria ♡

love notes

THANK YOU FOR BEING A FRIEND!

**Andrews McMeel
Publishing**

Kansas City

CD included featuring Andrew Gold

Photographs by Steve Bloom Images

Thank you for being a friend,

travelled down

a road...

and back again.

your heart is true,

you're a pal

and a confidant

I'm not ashamed to say,

I hope it always

will stay this way.

my hat is off

won't you stand

up and take a bow?

And if you threw a party,

invited everyone

you knew

you would see,

the biggest gift

would be from me.

and the card attached would say,

thank you for being a friend.

If it's a car you lack,

I'd surely buy you a Cadillac,

whatever you need any time

of the day or night.

I'm not **ashamed** to say,

I hope it always

will stay this way,

My hat is off,

won't you stand up and take a bow?

And when we both get **older**, with walking canes and hair of grey,

have no fear even though

it's hard to hear,

I will stand real close and say,

thank you for
being a friend.

And when we die,
and float away,
into the night,
the Milky Way,
you'll hear me call,
as we ascend,
I'll say your name,
then once again...

thank you for being a friend.

Steve Bloom

Like much of the wildlife that Steve Bloom photographs, he, too, is a rare species. It takes an uncommon blend of skill, knowledge, tenacity, energy and artistry to create evocative images of the natural world.

Born in South Africa in 1953, Steve moved to England in 1977 where he established a photographic special effects company. During the nineties he swapped his established career for the precarious life of freelance wildlife photographer, which demands an added measure of uncompromising passion and commitment. He has since won awards for his photography, and his first book, "*In Praise of Primates*", has been published in 10 languages.

Steve Bloom Images was established with the objective of offering clients high quality imagery. Now representing other wildlife photographers, the images are widely published throughout the world as calendars, posters, fine art prints, and in advertising.

www.stevebloom.com

Photographs © Steve Bloom and Pete Oxford

"Thank You For Being A Friend"
Written by Andrew Gold

Published by Zomba Enterprises Inc. and used with kind permission
by BMG Publishing Australia Pty Ltd.

Published in 2004 by PQ Publishers Limited,
Studio 3.11, Axis Building, 1 Cleveland Road, Parnell, Auckland, New Zealand.
www.pqpublishers.com

This edition published in North America in 2004 by
Andrews McMeel Publishing
4520 Main Street
Kansas City, MO 64111-7701

Printed by Midas Printing, China

ISBN: 0-7407-4394-5

PQ

Thank you for being a friend, travelled down a road and back again, your heart is true, you're a pal and a confidant. I'm not ashamed to say, I hope it always will stay this way, my hat is off, won't you stand up and take a bow. And if you threw a party, invited everyone you knew, you would see, the biggest gift would be from me, and the card attached would say, thank you for being a friend. If it's a car you lack, I'd surely buy you a Cadillac, whatever you need any time of the day or night. I'm not ashamed to say, I hope it always will stay this way, my hat is off, won't you stand up and take a bow. And when we both get older, with walking canes and hair of grey, have no fear even though it's hard to hear, I will stand real close and say, thank you for being a friend. And when we die, and float away, into the night, the Milky Way, you'll hear me call, as we ascend, I'll say your name, then once again... thank you for being a friend. Thank you for being a friend, travelled down a road and back again, your heart is true, you're a pal and a confidant. I'm not ashamed to say, I hope it always will stay this way, my hat is off, won't you stand up and take a bow. And if you threw a party, invited everyone you knew, you would see, the biggest gift would be from me, and the card attached would say, thank you for being a friend. If it's a car you lack, I'd surely buy you a Cadillac, whatever you need any time of the day or night. I'm not ashamed to say, I hope it always will stay this way, my hat is off, won't you stand up and take a bow. And when we both get older, with walking canes and hair of grey, have no fear even though it's hard to hear, I will stand real close and say, thank you for being a friend. And when we die, and float away, into the night, the Milky Way, you'll hear me call, as we ascend, I'll say your name, then once again... thank you for being a friend. Thank you for being a friend, travelled down a road and back again, your heart is true, you're a pal and a confidant. I'm not ashamed to say, I hope it always will stay this way, my hat is off, won't you stand up and take a bow. And if you threw a party, invited everyone you knew, you would see, the biggest gift would be from me, and the card attached would say, thank you for being a friend. If it's a car you lack, I'd surely buy you a Cadillac, whatever you need any time of the day or night. I'm not ashamed to say, I hope it always will stay this way, my hat is off, won't you stand up and take a bow. And when we both get older, with walking canes and hair of grey, have no fear even though it's hard to hear, I will stand real close and say, thank you for being a friend. And when we die, and float away, into the night, the Milky Way, you'll hear me call, as we ascend, I'll say your name, then once again... thank you for being a friend. Thank you for being a friend, travelled down a road and back again, your heart is true, you're a pal and a confidant. I'm not ashamed to say, I hope it always will stay this way, my hat is off, won't you stand up and take a bow. And if you threw a party, invited everyone you knew, you would see, the biggest gift would be from me, and the card attached would say, thank you for being a friend. If it's a car you lack, I'd surely buy you a Cadillac, whatever you need any time of the day or night. I'm not ashamed to say, I hope it always will stay this way, my hat is off, won't you stand up and take a bow. And when we both get older, with walking canes and hair of grey, have no fear even though it's hard to hear, I will stand real close and say, thank you for being a friend. And when we die, and float away, into the night, the Milky Way, you'll hear me call, as we ascend, I'll say your name, then once again... thank you for being a friend. And when we die, and float away, into the night,